Spitfire

The complete history of an icon of the skies

igloobooks

igloobooks

Published in 2015
by Igloo Books Ltd
Cottage Farm
Sywell
NN6 0BJ
www.igloobooks.com

Images supplied courtesy of Getty Images.

SHE001 0714
4 6 8 10 9 7 5 3
ISBN 978-1-78197-924-2

Distributed in association with G2 Entertainment Limited

Printed and manufactured in China

Spitfire

The complete history of an icon of the skies

Contents

Creator Of A Legend

the Sea Lion II: this aircraft proved victorious in the 1922 Schneider Trophy, thereby denying the Italians an outright third win, as they had already won the previous two events. The Sea Lion II, flown by Henri Biard, won at an average speed of 145.72mph.

The success of the Americans in the 1923 races at Cowes, Isle of Wight, was food for thought for R J Mitchell. He had long been an admirer of the designs of Glenn Curtiss, an American who specialised in water-borne aircraft. The Blackburn Pellet, and the Supermarine Sea Lion III had been chosen to defend the trophy on behalf of the host country. The Pellet sank during the sea navigability section of the competition, leaving the Sea Lion to compete as the sole British representative. Ultimately, it finished third, behind two Curtiss CR3s from the USA. The winning aircraft, flown by US Navy Lt David Rittenhouse, averaged 177.39mph, more than 26mph faster than Mitchell's design: this massive speed differential caused the Briton to rethink his design strategy.

Hitherto, the Supermarine designs had all been based on the biplane flying boat principle, with a boat-style hull. While this generally resulted in fairly good sea behaviour, it was not an ideal configuration for high-speed aerial progress. The winning Curtiss CR3, and its compatriot the Wright NW2 (which sank during the same 1923 event), were also biplanes but with the major difference that they were float-planes, each having a slender fuselage, strut-mounted above twin floats. They also differed in the placement of the engine and propeller: the Supermarine design featured a pusher propeller driven by a non-cowled Napier Lion engine that was mounted below the upper wing, and with a large radiator mounted below

MAIN
Flt Lt D'Arcy
Greig in his
Supermarine S5
N219 in which
he attempted to
break the world
air speed record

MAIN
WWII Spitfire in a Sunset
Ceremony to mark
70th Anniversary of the
Dambuster Raid.

MAIN
Engineers testing
the engine of a
Supermarine S6B.

the front of the wing; the Curtiss CR3 was
powered by a closely-cowled engine, fitted
in the aircraft's nose, driving a tractor-style
propeller. Although both designs had engines
that produced a similar power output, the
Curtiss design was visibly "cleaner" and looked
much faster than the cluttered appearance
of the British-built Sea Lion flying boat.

Mitchell set about designing a new contender,
adopting the float-plane principle. His first,
unsuccessful attempt to regain the Schneider
Trophy for Britain was the Supermarine S4.
The designation "S", used to identify this
series of high-speed aircraft is often attributed
to the company name, Supermarine: however,
authoritative sources claim that it relates to
"Schneider", as the sole purpose of these
aircraft was to enter and, hopefully, win the
Schneider Trophy races. The S4 was a slim-
fuselage monoplane with twin floats, and was
powered by a 700hp Napier Lion engine. Its
appearance in the 1925 series, held in the USA,
was less than glorious: during a high-speed
test flight, the S4 developed aileron flutter and
crashed into the waters of Chesapeake Bay, off
Baltimore, Maryland. Fortunately, the pilot,
Henri Biard, survived the impact. The British
challenge was left to the Gloster III, piloted by
Hubert Broad, who finished in second place
at an average speed of just over 199mph. The
American winner was a Curtiss R2C-2 of the
US Army Air Service, piloted by 1st Lt James H
Doolittle, at an average speed of 232.573mph.

Lessons learned from the S4 were used
to great effect in the S5 programme. By this
time, Mitchell had also been granted the twin
benefits of the use of the wind tunnel at the
Royal Aircraft Establishment, Farnborough, and
the marine test tank facility at the National

MAIN
Aircraft K5054, the prototype for Spitfire fighter planes, designed by Reginald Mitchell, during a demonstration flight at Eastleigh

Creator Of A Legend

Physical Laboratory. The S4 project itself had not been a total disaster: it was a very advanced design with its cantilever monoplane wing, a 680hp Napier Lion VII engine, and formed the basis for Mitchell's next challenger, the Supermarine S5, for the 1927 series of races. For this series, in Venice, the Americans had withdrawn, leaving it as a head-to-head contest between Italy and Great Britain. The RAF High Speed Flight represented their country, having been established in May 1927. It had been originally proposed that the Napier Lion engine, now developing 900hp, would be replaced in the S5 by a Rolls-Royce engine: it was, however, decided to keep the Napier engine for the Venice event.

Three S5s, serial numbers N219, N220 and N221, were built. A radical departure from that of the S4 design was the use of wing bracing wires; this, together with the change from fabric to metal cladding on the ailerons, solved the wing flutter problem that had resulted in the S4 crash at Baltimore. The slim, streamlined fuselage left precious little space for the pilot, let alone for fuel. Mitchell's solution was to use the starboard float to store the fuel, gaining the additional benefits of lowering the centre of gravity and improving stability in flight. Radiators in the wings provided engine cooling. The S5 was triumphant, N220 winning the 1927 event at an average speed of 281.65mph, with N219 finishing second.

By 1929, the Rolls-Royce R engine was producing significantly more horsepower than the Napier, and was selected to power the Supermarine S6 for Britain's defence of the trophy. Mitchell set to and designed the S6 around the new engine. This necessitated the whole of the wing structure, except for the

ailerons, being used to contain the engine's liquid coolant, and pipes within corrugated fairings along the sides of the fuselage provided the cooling for the engine oil. Because of its importance in helping to keep the engine

BELOW
A Supermarine S6B
outside its hangar.

cool, the S6 was sometimes referred to, by its designer, as "the flying radiator". The floats were also redesigned using data from Mitchell's aerodynamic and hydrodynamic testing. Mitchell's radical design paid off: the

Schneider Trophy stayed in Britain, the event being won by S6 serial number N247, flown by Flying Officer H R Waghorn at a speed of 328.63mph, with S6 number N248 in second place, although this aircraft was later

MAIN
A formation
of Spitfires.

disqualified for missing a course marker.

Britain won the Schneider Trophy outright after a third consecutive win in 1931. Mitchell's development of the 1929 aircraft was designated the S6B, and two new airframes were built, serial numbers S1595 and S1596. The two 1929 aircraft were modified to the same standard, and designated S6A. By this time, the R engine was producing over 2,000hp. In the race, S1595 was victorious, at an average speed of 340mph. Later, an S6B set a new world air speed record at 407.5mph. In 1932, Mitchell was awarded the CBE for his contribution towards Britain's

achievements in the world of high-speed flight.

In spite of his success in the world of aviation, Mitchell was not particularly well-known outside that sphere of activity, being an intensely private man who shunned all personal publicity. His personal qualities of kindness and humanity towards those with whom he came into contact, particularly within the Supermarine company, earned the respect and affection of his staff and colleagues. His resolute nature came to the fore in 1933, when he was diagnosed with cancer of the bowel. After a major operation, he refused to give up his

work, and continued with his design activities: he was working on the plans for a new fighter aircraft, utilising his experiences in the Schneider Trophy: Mitchell had also started preliminary design work on a new bomber project.

The bomber never materialised, as the plans for it, and a wooden mock-up, were lost when German bombs destroyed much of the Supermarine works early in the war. Prior to his death on 11 June 1937, at the age of 42, he had seen the fruits of his labours on the fighter project take to the skies. He did not live to see how important his contribution was to prove,

in the dark years of conflict that were soon to follow. In a BBC Midlands television poll in 2003, R J Mitchell was voted the "Greatest Midlander of all Time", beating William Shakespeare into second place. Long after his death, his achievements have been recognised by the erection of a statue in his honour, and civic buildings have been given his name, the citizens of his home town rightfully acknowledging his importance in British aviation history.

MAIN
The winning English Schneider Trophy team in front of the Supermarine S6B, 1931.

Chapter Two

Taming
the
Shrew

Taming The Shrew

If things had turned out differently, the aircraft that became known as the Spitfire could possibly have been named Shrew, or Shrike, as these were among the names proposed by the Air Ministry for their new fighter aircraft. In 1930, they issued a specification for a new day and night fighter, armed with four machine guns: Supermarine were among those companies that were interested in becoming involved in the project; in due course, Mitchell designed the Supermarine Type 224 to meet that specification.

The result was an unlikely-looking, open-cockpit aeroplane of stressed-skin construction, with an inverted gull wing, no wing flaps, and a fixed undercarriage housed in trouser-like fairings. The 660hp Rolls-Royce Goshawk engine gave a design speed of 228mph: engine cooling was by the method used in the S-series Schneider Trophy aircraft, the leading edges of the gull wing acting as condensers, with the collector tanks for the condensed water being housed in the trouser fairings. Only one prototype was built: a combination of factors resulted in the contract for the fighter being awarded to Gloster for a derivative of the Gauntlet fighter, the Gladiator, which was destined to become the last biplane fighter to be ordered by the RAF.

Much of the criticism of the Type 224 was levelled at the choice of engine. Although the Air Ministry suggested that the most modern engines should be considered in all new-design aircraft, this was never stipulated in the contract. The eventual winner, the Gladiator, and the Bristol Type 133 contender that was later to be lost in an accident, were both powered by a more traditional, air-cooled radial engine, the Bristol Mercury. The Type 224 did not offer a significant performance increase over its

MAIN
Training getting underway.

Taming The Shrew

RIGHT
Diagram of a
Spitfire Mark XI.

MAIN
A Battle of Britain
type "scramble".
An improved
Spitfire is pushed
onto the runway by
a group of pilots
from the squadron.

rivals; its climb rate was inferior to that of the Gladiator, it was technically more complex, and its flapless configuration gave it a much higher landing speed than its biplane competitor.

Even before the rejection of the Type 224, Mitchell had commenced his next project, the Supermarine Type 300. For this new design, it was intended to again use the Goshawk engine, so the wing leading edges were designed to act as condensation tanks for the cooling system. When the Rolls-Royce PV-12 engine, later to be known as the Merlin, became available, it was initially proposed that it should be steam-cooled, so the condensation system was retained, supplemented by a small radiator. Later in the development of the Merlin, the unreliability of the steam cooling system led to this being discarded, being replaced initially by a more efficient pressurised all-liquid, ethylene glycol system, later changed to a water/ethylene glycol mixture system.

The Air Ministry specification called for a minimum speed, in level flight, of at least 195mph, with a service ceiling of not less than 28,000ft. A further rate of climb stipulation was that the aircraft should reach 15,000ft in eight and a half minutes, or less. No preference for

MAIN
Spitfire MJ730
was known
as the "CO's
Query" due to
its unusual unit
code marking.

either a biplane or monoplane was specified. Provision was to be made for the carriage of full oxygen and wireless equipment, and the fighter should be capable of day and night operations. With the amended specification taking into account the design features of Mitchell's latest offering, the Type 300 eventually met

all the physical requirements: although the design calculations indicated compliance with the specified criteria, the performance could only be demonstrated in flight.

The strengthened wing leading edge was no longer required for cooling purposes; however, it was retained, and formed an integral part of the

MAIN
K5054, the Spitfire prototype during a demonstration flight at Eastleigh.

wing structure. The wing design incorporated a hollow, square-section main spar boom built up from five sections that slotted into each other. Two of these spar booms were connected by an alloy spar web, the whole spar assembly giving the wing strength and resilience. The leading edge skin was flush riveted, thereby improving air flow and reducing drag; to the rear of the main spar, the top skin was secured by domed rivets. Some parts of the lower skin were originally fixed by wood screws, into spruce sections, but this method was later changed to pop-riveting into metalwork.

MAIN
The press taking an interest in K5054, the Spitfire prototype.

MAIN
The Spitfire
production line
at the Vickers
Supermarine Works
in Southampton.

front of the unfortunate aviator. Coupled with the close confines of the cockpit, that made entry and egress difficult at best, many pilots made an adrenaline-fuelled exit through flames and smoke; many were badly burned in the process.

Unlike that of the Hurricane, the fuselage was of monocoque construction, a method that had been proven in the Supermarine S-series of Schneider Trophy fame. The all-metal fuselage was made up from a series of oval-shaped frames, pierced with lightening holes, connected by two main longerons and a series of longitudinal stringers, all covered by a riveted stressed-skin cladding. This arrangement afforded the possibility for the installation of bulky camera equipment in later developments, although its relatively complex method of construction, compared to the tubular frame and fabric-covering of earlier types of fighter, caused problems in both manufacturing and in-service repair.

The Type 300 project was developed by Supermarine as a private venture, although the Air Ministry was aware of its existence: recognition of its potential as a front-line fighter was soon to come in the guise of Specification F10/35. This was written around the new aircraft design, taking into account its range limitations, and was soon followed by official funding for the building of the prototype. Ably assisted by the aerodynamicist, Beverley Shenstone, and his own familiar and trusted team of detail designers, Mitchell, by now a very sick man, devoted his last few working months to the project.

Construction of the prototype commenced in December 1934. The Air Ministry had allocated the registration K5054 to the first aircraft, probably one of the best-known serial numbers in the history of aviation. They had

also suggested a series of possible names for the aircraft: the usual policy was for the model name to begin with the same letter as that of the aircraft manufacturer, hence the list of possibles suggested by the ministry included Shrew, and Shrike. The final name selected by the company, that was now part of the Vickers organisation, is said to have been suggested by Sir Robert McLean, a director, who had often referred to his daughter Ann as being "a little spitfire". The word "spitfire" was in common usage in 16th century Britain, usually in the context of a female with a fiery spirit or temperament. Having previously been used, unofficially, for the Type 224, it was formally approved for the new fighter. R J Mitchell's reaction was that it was "just the sort of bloody silly name they would choose".

Visually, the Spitfire was a beautiful and well-proportioned aircraft. With a length of 30ft, wingspan of 37ft and being just over 8ft high, it weighed 5359lb. Its fixed-pitch propeller was driven by a Rolls-Royce Merlin engine that had an output of 990hp. Its clean lines differed markedly from the generation of biplane fighters that were in current front-line service. Apart from its two-bladed propeller, a tail skid instead of a tailwheel, and the lack of undercarriage doors, the prototype would, today, still be instantly recognisable as a Spitfire, had it survived. Keen spotters will note that there was a horizontal horn balance at the top of the rudder, and the cockpit canopy was flush fitting rather than the bulged shape on later versions. Apart from these relatively minor details, the Spitfire's distinctive outline remained largely unchanged throughout much of its lengthy production run. The pace of development was such that there was no time to apply a paint finish prior to the maiden flight. By early March of 1936, the series of ground tests and engine runs had been completed, and the necessary certification had been signed off by the Aeronautical Inspection Directorate. The Spitfire was ready to take to the skies.

The first flight of the Spitfire prototype K5054 took place at Eastleigh, now known as Southampton Airport, on 5 March 1936, piloted by Joseph "Mutt" Summers, the Vickers chief test pilot. This vastly experienced pilot, who carried out the first flight of over 40 different aircraft types in a test-flying career of over 30 years, certainly knew his aeroplanes: after the flight he was reported to have said that it had "handled beautifully" and to the engineers said, "don't touch a thing!", a testament to the design skills of Mitchell and his team. The maiden flight had lasted around eight minutes. In the next few days, Summers carried out further tests, gradually exploring the flight envelope with a series of steep turns and stalls, amassing one hour and 44 minutes of flight time in three days.

Subsequently, the Spitfire achieved a speed of 349mph. Further test flight results proved that this was going to be an outstanding aircraft, and its promise was rewarded by the Air Ministry placing an order for 310 aircraft, on 3 June 1936, even before the test programme had been completed. Over the next few weeks, flight testing continued without major problems and, on 26 May 1936, K5054 was handed over to the Aeroplane and Armament Experimental Establishment at Martlesham Heath for her official trials. Resulting from these trials, minor refinements to the design were made, bringing the prototype up to the standard that effectively became the pattern for the first production version.

Undercarriage door fairings and a tailwheel in place of the skid were the more obvious visual changes made to the production aircraft.

Things did not run altogether smoothly during the flight trials: on 22 March 1937, the Merlin lost its oil pressure and K5054 was damaged when it made a forced belly landing on open heathland in Suffolk. After repairs, the flight tests continued. The main problems in the flight testing phase centred on the controls, particularly wing flutter at high speeds. Minor changes to the control system, together with the change to the use of an all-metal skin covering for the ailerons instead of the previous fabric, cured this particular defect.

One fateful day followed another: on 3 September 1939, Britain declared war on Germany; the following day saw K5054 destroyed in a crash at the Royal Aircraft Establishment, Farnborough, when it nosed over on landing. The pilot, Flt Lt White, died of injuries received when the mast that was situated to the rear of the cockpit, was pushed downwards through the fuselage with such force that it took the Sutton seat harness anchor with it, bending the backrest of the pilot's seat rearwards in the impact. Lesson learned, the seat harness anchor cable was attached to the rear fuselage structure in production aircraft.

However, the gestation period of the Spitfire was almost complete; her baptism of fire was about to take place. The era of the British monoplane piston-engined fighter had begun; few at the time had any idea of the importance of this aircraft, both in military terms, and the uplifting effect on the morale of the British nation in the dark days of war. Neither did they have any reason to believe that the Spitfire would still be in RAF service for a period of around 15 years.

Chapter Three
Evolution of an Icon

Evolution of an Icon

The name of R J Mitchell will always be associated with the design of the Spitfire. Unfortunately, he only lived long enough to see his creation take its maiden flight before his untimely death, some 15 months later. The onerous task of developing the Spitfire fell to his chief draughtsman, Joseph "Joe" Smith, who had succeeded Mitchell as chief designer. Smith was responsible for keeping the Spitfire at the cutting edge of Britain's fighter force, his expertise being reflected in the accolade given by an aviation historian who wrote, "If Mitchell was born to design the Spitfire, Joe Smith was born to defend and develop it": this he did to great effect. During its service life, the weight of the Spitfire increased by more than half, its engine power more than doubled, and its top speed rose by between 25 and 30 percent, compared to that of the first version to enter service.

Joseph Smith was reported, on several occasions, as having said at design meetings and elsewhere that "… the good big 'un will eventually beat the good little 'un", with particular reference to aircraft engines. Although the Merlin was an exceptional engine, Smith believed that the Griffon, with its much greater capacity of 36 litres, against the 27 litres of the Merlin, had more potential for development, as the Merlin had been taken almost to the practical limit of its power output. He had wanted the Griffon to be installed in the Spitfire as early as 1940, but the military circumstances, later known as the Battle of Britain, caused this to be deferred until the spring of 1941. Before the end of that year the first Griffon engine, a Griffon IIB with a single-stage supercharger, was installed in what was basically a modified Spitfire Mark III airframe, now designated as a Spitfire Mark IV, serial

number DP845, and made its first flight with Jeffrey Quill at the controls on 27 November 1941, from Worthy Down Aerodrome.

In all, there were 24 distinct marks of Spitfire, and many sub-variants. Differences between marks were largely defined by their engine and propeller, Merlin or Griffon, with propellers ranging from the fixed-pitch, two-bladed version of the prototype and early production versions, to the contra-rotating, six-bladed installation of the Seafire 47. A series of different wing and armament arrangements, known as the A, B, C, or E wings, were used across the various marks and derivatives. The "A" wing housed eight 0.303in machine guns and lacked the large bulge on the upper surface, distinguishing it from the cannon-equipped types; the "B" wing had four 0.303in machine guns and two 20mm Hispano cannon, the "C" (or commonly, "Universal" wing) could be fitted with either four 20mm cannon or two 20mm cannon and four 0.303in machine guns, and the "E" variation had two 20mm cannon and two 0.50in Browning heavy machine guns. Later in its development, a laminar flow wing was introduced in order to improve high-speed performance, but this development was overtaken by the introduction of the jet fighter into RAF service and did not enter full production.

Not all marks of Spitfire were built from scratch: some were converted during build, or from earlier production aircraft, making things somewhat complicated for the uninitiated to understand. Even the method of numbering the different marks was changed, as the design progressed; earlier versions were numbered in Roman numerals but, from the Mark 21 onwards, the numbers were given in Arabic numerals. Some references to the Marks XVIII and XIX also used Arabic numerals, many eminent Spitfire authorities disagree over which is the correct form. In some cases, a suffix letter was added, usually to signify the wing type variation within that particular mark, and other versions with specialist tasks, such as the photo reconnaissance or fighter reconnaissance Spitfires, were given the prefix PR or FR followed by the mark number.

Type 300–Spitfire Mark I. This was the first production version and entered RAF service with Nos 19 and 66 Squadrons in 1938. With its Merlin II engine giving 1,030hp at 16,250ft, it had an official top speed of 347mph but, with the addition of a bullet-proof windscreen and armour plating for pilot protection, it was probably somewhat slower by around 20mph. Early aircraft had a flush-topped canopy; later deliveries had the bulged,

Malcolm-type of bubble canopy. The de Havilland three-bladed movable-pitch propeller replaced the original fixed-pitch unit. Two variants, the Mark IA and Mark IB made up the total of 1,566 produced. The Mark I was the mainstay of the Spitfire force during the Battle of Britain, although some Mark IIs were also in service. Even so, the Hawker Hurricane was in service in much greater numbers.

Speed Spitfire. A world speed record attempt was to be made with two modified versions of the Mark I. K9834 was fitted with a special version of the Merlin, short-span wings, and a streamlined cockpit canopy. The attempt was abandoned when the Germans put the record out of reach, so the aircraft was fitted with a standard Merlin XII and used as a high-speed reconnaissance aircraft.

Type 329–Mark II. Fitted with the Merlin XII delivering 1,175hp that gave a top speed increase of some 10mph. Mark IIA and IIB versions were produced in great numbers at Castle Bromwich, as the Supermarine factory at Southampton had been badly damaged by enemy bombing. In all, 750 Mark IIA and 170 Mark IIB Spitfires were built.

Type 348–Mark III. Experimental version powered by a 1,280hp Merlin XX with two-speed supercharger, constant-speed propeller, modified windscreen, retractable tailwheel, and clipped wings. Only one was built, and mainly used as a test airframe for the Merlin 61 engine.

Note. Early reconnaissance versions of the Spitfire were originally designated with a letter suffix, A to F, but this was changed in 1941 to the Roman numeral style, when they became PR Marks I to VI. A great many were converted from Mark IA fighter aircraft and were stripped of all armament, and fitted with a variety of aerial cameras. Extended range fuel and oil tanks were added. Later versions of the PRs were numbered similarly to the fighter designations.

Type 353-Mark IV. This was a single prototype for the later, Griffon-powered, Spitfires. After further modification, it became the Mark XX.

Type 349-Mark V. Powered by several versions of the Merlin engine, and three different wing types, this mark was produced in greater numbers than any other previous Spitfire. Some had clipped wings and more powerful engines fitted, for improved low-level performance, drop tanks could be fitted for increased range, and many Mark Vs could carry 250 or 500lb bombs. This mark served with particular distinction in Europe; it was similarly successful in the North Africa campaign and elsewhere, although its specially-adapted, and rather prominent, engine intake dust filter housing somewhat spoiled the classic Spitfire outline on the out-of-Europe version. Including the PR Mark V, production totalled 6,693.

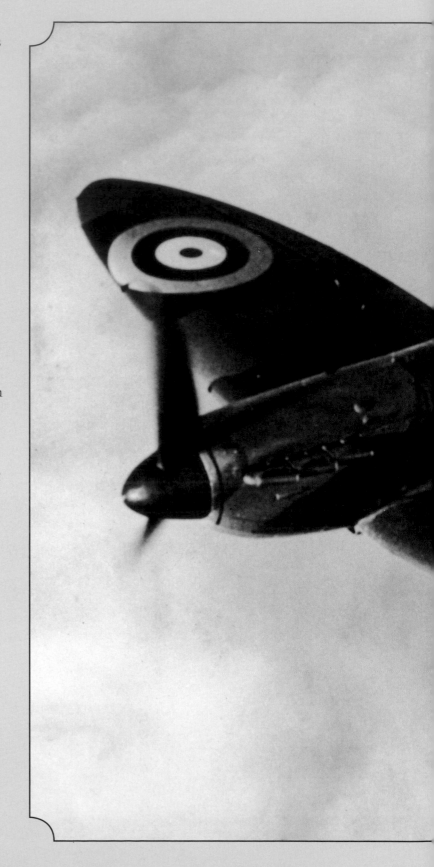

MAIN
A Spitfire Mark I.

MAIN
Spitfire in
flight, 1946.

Evolution of an Icon

Type 350–Mark VI. This high-altitude variant had a 1,415hp Merlin 47, driving a four-bladed propeller, and extended, rather pointed wing tips. Developed to combat the threat of high altitude, enemy reconnaissance aircraft and bombers, this mark was fitted with a partly-pressurised cockpit and had a service ceiling of 41,000ft. The "B" type wing housed its armament of two cannon and four machine guns. Production as 100 aircraft.

Type 351–Mark VII. Powered by the Merlin 60-series engines that introduced the two-speed, two-stage supercharger, this version differed visually in that it had symmetrical radiators under each wing, rather than the asymmetric radiator and oil cooler arrangement of earlier marks, and an enlarged rudder with a pointed tip. Production totalled 140.

Type 360–Mark VIII. In essence, an unpressurised Mark VII, with a Merlin 61

MAIN
Supermarine
Spitfire Mark PRXI.

MAIN
The elliptical planform of a Mark V.

or 63 (1,565 or 1,710hp) and a four-bladed propeller. Carburettor modifications permitted negative g manoeuvring, thus improving previous shortcomings in aerial combat. Many of the 1,652 built were modified for tropical use, and one was later adapted to become what would have been the first two-seat Spitfire, but this option was not pursued during the war.

Type 361–Mark IX. Developed around a strengthened Mark V airframe, this version had a Merlin 60-series engine and four-bladed propeller, and several differing wing and armament arrangements. It started out as a short term fix, to counter the threat of the Focke-Wulf 190, and eventually became a major success, with a total of 5,665 built. In its

LEFT
RB518, a Type
393-Spiteful.

two main variations, one for low altitude with clipped wings, and the other with extended wing tips for high altitude, in addition to the standard fighter version, the Mark IX formed the backbone of the RAF air campaign over Europe.

Type 362-Mark PRX. Based on a converted Mark VII airframe, only 16 were produced, some without the pressurised cockpit. Optimised for high-altitude photo reconnaissance, this unarmed version had a retractable tailwheel, Merlin 64 or 71-series engine, leading edge fuel tanks, and a larger oil tank for increased range. Various camera installations were used.

Type 365-Mark PRXI. Similar to the PRX, but without pressurisation. Fitted with tropical equipment as standard, 461 were built. This out-of-sequence variant actually appeared before the PRX.

Type 366-Mark XII. A significant change with the introduction of the Griffon II or IV, giving some 1,720hp. Another radical difference was that the four-bladed propeller of the Griffon rotated in the opposite direction to Merlin-powered aircraft. Most were clipped-

wing variants, and had a retractable tailwheel. 100 were built. Very fast, it was credited with destroying several V1 flying bombs.

Mark PRXIII. Similar to the Mark V, as it used the same camera system, but with the Merlin 32 engine that had been optimised for low-level flight. Fitted with only four machine guns, this mark played a significant part in the Normandy campaign.

Type 373-Mark XIV. Based on the Mark VIII, 957 were built, powered by the Griffon 65 that, by now, developed in excess of 2,000hp. A five-bladed propeller, and a larger fin and rudder, were obvious differences. Later a cut-down rear fuselage, to allow for the new, improved-visibility tear-drop canopy was introduced. With two differing wing and armament types, this mark was often used against ground targets when fitted with a 250 or 500lb bomb under the fuselage. It was also fast enough to intercept the infamous V1 flying bomb, on many occasions.

Type 361-Mark XVI. Built alongside the Mark IX, 1,054 were produced with the American-built Packard Merlin 266 driving a four-bladed propeller. Two wing types were fitted, some having wing tip extensions, later batches had clipped wings and a cut-down rear fuselage with the tear-drop canopy.

Type 394-Mark XVIII (Otherwise Mark 18). Redesigned Mark VIII airframe to take the Griffon 63 (2,035hp) or 65 (2,375hp) engine. All 300 built had the tear-drop canopy and an increased fuel capacity.

Type 390-Mark PRXIX (Also known as PR19). Unarmed version based on fuselage of the Mark XIV with a pressurised cockpit, except for the first 22 of the 225 built. Its top speed of 445mph and a service ceiling of 42,600ft made it almost immune from enemy attack. The PRXIX entered RAF service in May 1944 and made the last operational RAF sortie on 1 April 1954. It remained in service on meteorological work at RAF Woodvale until June 1957.

Type 356-Mark 21. First version to be designated from the outset with Arabic numerals, this mark, although similar in appearance to earlier Spitfires, was a major redesign. Its long nose was typical of the Griffon-powered versions, but its Type C armament wing, with four 20mm cannon, was effectively a complete redesign, with a differently shaped outer wing that was no longer elliptical in plan form. It had an increased span with longer ailerons, and was, structurally, much stiffer. 122 were built.

Type 356-Mark 22. In effect, a Mark 21 with a cut-down rear fuselage and tear-drop canopy. With C or E wing variations, 278 were produced.

Type 356-Mark 24. Similar to the Mark 22, the 54 aircraft built were fitted with the short-barrelled Hispano cannon. Some were also fitted with rocket-rails on their "C" pattern wings.

This version featured the Griffon 64 engine that was, by now, giving an output of 2,340hp.

Type 393-Spiteful. A radical development that combined a Spitfire fuselage, a Griffon engine, and a newly-designed laminar flow wing that was believed to give a better high-speed performance. Two early development prototypes were converted from Spitfire Mark XIVs, and kept the original Spitfire tail assembly. The first production prototype had the new wing that also housed a radically redesigned, inwards-retracting undercarriage, and a new tail assembly with an increased area to the fin, rudder and tailplane. There were a number of problems with this new aircraft and, with the advent of jet aircraft, and the imminent ending of hostilities, the Spiteful project was cancelled.

Type 509-Trainer (Tr) Mark IX. After hostilities ceased, Vickers-Armstrong bought back a small number of Mark IX Spitfires, in order to satisfy a strong overseas demand for the aircraft. It was deemed necessary to produce a two-seat trainer version to meet pilot training requirements, although this luxury had not been afforded to the wartime RAF pilots! A total of 26 two-seat Spitfires were produced, wherein the front cockpit was moved forwards, and a second cockpit with a raised seat, domed canopy, and dual-controls, added behind it. Supermarine produced the first official Spitfire two-seater as a private venture, using a Mark VIII as the basis for conversion. In the Middle East, a locally-modified Mark V was flown by No 261 Squadron in 1946; this aircraft could carry a passenger but its rear cockpit was bereft of any flying controls. During the war, the Soviet Union had also produced some two-seat conversions but these were not officially classed as Tr Mark IXs.

MAIN
A Spitfire is
sillouhetted against
the sky during an
aerial display.

The Power and the Growler

Chapter Four
The Power and the Growler

The Power and the Growler

The Spitfire, in its many variations, was powered by two main types of engine, first the Merlin and later, the Griffon, both designed by the Rolls-Royce company. Their names followed the customary practice whereby all of the company's piston aero-engines were given the names of birds of prey. Although having a similar appearance, both being liquid-cooled 12-cylinder engines arranged in "V" configuration with six cylinders in each bank, there were considerable differences between the two. Both engines drew heavily on the Rolls-Royce company's experience of high-powered engine design gained from their participation in the Schneider Trophy race: success in this event had ensured the company's continued long association with aero-engines that had begun in WW1, during which conflict they had produced some 60 percent of all British aircraft engines.

In the 1920s, the Fairey Aviation Company, together with the Air Ministry, were not particularly enamoured with the American engine, the Curtiss D-12, which was installed in the Fairey Fox light bomber. The D-12 had been used in the victorious American aircraft, the Curtiss CR-3, in the 1923 Schneider Trophy races and, subsequently, in the Curtiss R3C-2 for the 1925 event. It was a liquid-cooled, in-line V12, and had a capacity of 18.7 litres. Given its racing pedigree, the main reason for the lack of enthusiasm for the D-12 was that it only produced a relatively meagre 375hp, although this was later increased to 435hp. Due to its configuration as a direct-drive engine, where the propeller rotated at the same speed as the engine crankshaft, and the engine's relatively small internal capacity, there were obvious limitations to its development, as it had relied heavily on the highly specialised aerodynamics of the propeller for its success as a racing engine.

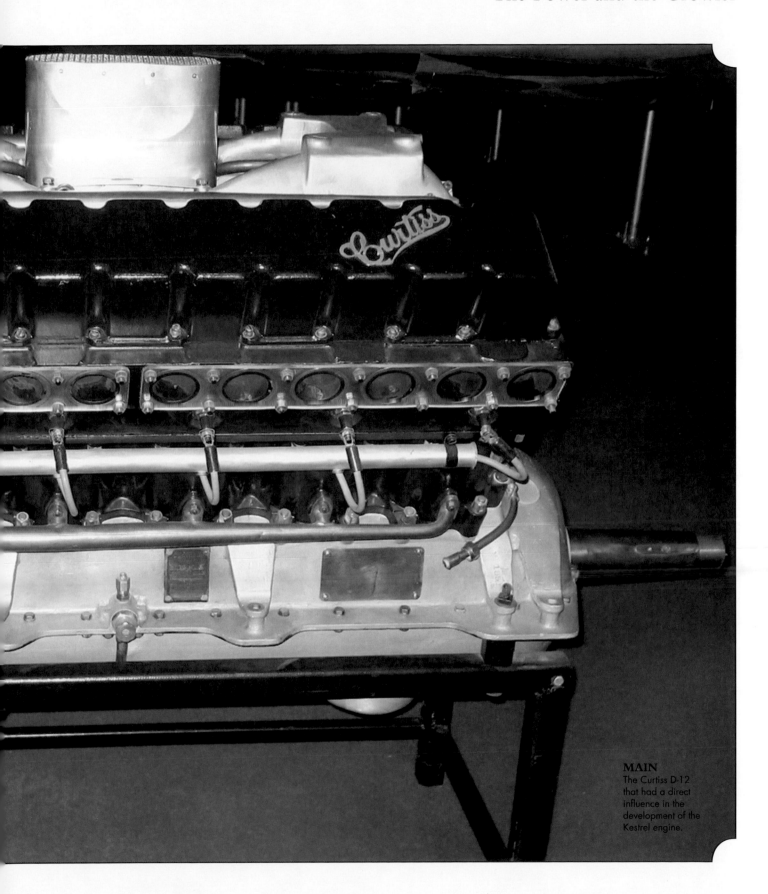

MAIN
The Curtiss D-12
that had a direct
influence in the
development of the
Kestrel engine.

MAIN
The R-type Schneider Trophy engine at the Rolls-Royce works in Derby.

MAIN
The Merlin engine that was much used in fighter planes during WW2.

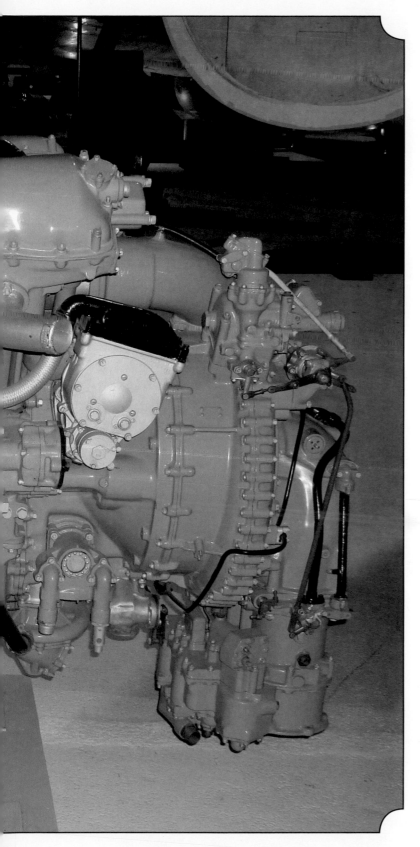

The Curtiss engine was sent to Rolls-Royce for evaluation and, as a result, the British company began to develop the Kestrel engine that was to supersede the D-12 in the Fairey Fox, and help to re-establish the British company in the forefront of aviation engine manufacturing. The requirement for a much higher power rating than the Kestrel's eventual output of around 745hp, for the Schneider Trophy aircraft, led to the development of the famous R-type ("R" signifying Racing), that used a custom-made high-performance fuel, coupled with supercharging. A supercharged engine has its fuel/air mixture compressed, thereby forcing a denser mixture into the cylinders; this has the effect of greatly increasing the engine's volumetric efficiency with the dual advantages of both significantly increasing the power output at lower altitudes and, importantly, improving or maintaining power output at higher altitudes, where that of a normally aspirated engine falls off markedly with an increase in altitude.

In its later stages of development, for the 1931 Supermarine S6B, the R-type produced a remarkable output of 2,783hp, although this was due largely to the use of expensive and highly specialised, methanol-based fuels; the engine also had a comparatively short operating life. These factors alone precluded the use of the R-type as a production engine, so the company embarked on a project to design a new high-performance engine that used a conventional 100-octane aviation fuel, would be reliable, and also have an acceptable operational lifespan. The result of their labours was destined to become, probably, the world's most famous piston aero-engine, the Rolls-Royce Merlin.

To fill the void between its 700hp Peregrine and 1,700hp Vulture engines, Rolls-Royce

The Power and the Growler

opted for a new engine design, aimed to fill a power output requirement of around 1,100hp, and be suitable for installation in a single-engined fighter. The new engine was given the designation PV-12 (Private Venture 12 cylinders), as no government funding was involved at this stage. It was originally envisaged that the cooling system would utilise the steam condensing principle but this was later rejected, due to its inherent unreliability and operational performance drawbacks. The company also used sodium-cooled exhaust valves that did much to reduce pre-ignition, thus enhancing the engine's performance and reliability.

The design of the PV-12 retained the cast block principle of the Kestrel engine, in which the cylinders were machined from a large block casting, rather than as individual items. Supercharging was a fundamental part of the design, as was the use of an unpressurised liquid cooling system that was filled with the newly available, and much more efficient, ethylene glycol. In later versions, cooling was achieved by a pressurised 70/30 percent water/ethylene glycol mixture that, apart from being more economical, afforded a lower boiling point at altitude; it also presented a much lower fire hazard in combat. With the eventual placement of a government contract, the newly-named Merlin went into production, but not before Rolls-Royce had incorporated many modifications, and built some 33 prototypes, culminating in the Merlin F that went into production with a rated power output of 1,035hp.

Early versions of the Merlin were first fitted in the Fairey Battle light bomber, and in the Hurricane fighter, although there were many problems with reliability. A far-reaching improvement programme involved

MAIN
A Rolls-Royce Kestrel engine.

The Power and the Growler

the random selection of an engine from the production line, then running it on the test bed, at full power, until it failed. Examination of the failed engine usually revealed the cause of the failure, resulting in redesign or strengthening of the offending component. The inclined valve arrangement, known as the "ramp-head" caused particular problems,

MAIN
A Packard-built
Merlin as used in
the P-51 Mustang.

and was replaced by the Kestrel-standard, flat-head arrangement. As a direct result of this improvement programme, the Merlin became one of the most reliable of all aero-engines.

Following on from the letter-designations of the prototypes, A to G, a numerical system was introduced for production versions. The F engine later became the Merlin I; the

MAIN
A Spitfire in the marking of 340 Squadron, (Free French).

The Power and the Growler

G-engine became the Merlin II, and appeared in 1938: it was followed by the Merlin III that drove the new constant-speed propeller. Together, these two versions were produced in large numbers, a total of over 9,700 being fitted in numerous RAF aircraft of the wartime period, from the Spitfire, Hurricane, Battle, and Boulton Paul Defiant I, to the Hawker Henley. With a single-speed, single-stage supercharger, the Merlin III had a capacity of 27 litres, a power output of 1,030hp at 3,000rpm, at an altitude of 5,500ft, and weighed 1,375lb.

Such was the importance of the Merlin to Britain's war effort that a set of plans was sent to America, for safe-keeping, to prevent their falling into enemy hands in the event of an invasion. In due course, the engine was built in large numbers, under licence, in the USA where it was known as the Packard Merlin, after the automotive company that was chosen because of its experience in mass-production engineering. Some parts were redesigned to meet American production standards and tooling methods, as well as allowing it to be assembled by a relatively unskilled workforce. One feature missing from the Packard-built Merlins was the inscription "Rolls-Royce" that appeared on each of the two camshaft covers on the British-built versions.

The Packard Merlin was used to great effect in the American P-51 Mustang fighter, that was also used by the RAF: in its V-1650-3 variant with a two-speed, two-stage supercharger, as installed in the P-51B & C models and the RAF's Mustang III, it produced 1,520hp. Its supercharger, as with all of the two-speed units, had an automatic speed changeover switch that increased the engine boost at a given altitude; there was also a manual override, limited to five minutes use, that could be initiated by the pilot in an emergency combat situation after first breaking a tell-tale wire fitted to the switch.

The success of the Spitfire, and the Hurricane, in the early years of the war was largely due to the performance and reliability of the Merlin, which went on to famously power the Lancaster and Mosquito in their particular spheres of operations. The Merlin had been developed to such an extent that, in its later versions, it was producing around twice the power output of the Spitfire Mark I's Merlin III (1,030hp); the two-speed, two-stage supercharged Merlin 130 had a low-altitude output of 2,030hp, and delivered around 1,000hp at altitudes up to 36,000ft. In 1944, a Merlin was reputed to have produced an almost unbelievable 2,640hp, for 15 minutes, on the test bed. Power indeed!

Quite early in the Merlin project, it was believed that there would be a limit to its development, based on the somewhat erroneous premise that its engine capacity of 27 litres would be incapable of producing a significant increase in power, beyond that of its original design calculation. At that time, advances in supercharging design had not reached the levels that were incorporated in later versions of the Merlin, particularly the introduction of the two-stage, two-speed supercharger. Traditionally, the recognised method of increasing the power output of an engine was to increase its swept volume. Although its greater size would also lead to an increase in weight, the potential for increased power output was a key factor in the choice of a larger engine. Enter, the Griffon.

The prototype Griffon was built in 1934. Born out of the engine that had brought success in the Schneider Trophy it was, to all intents and purposes, a de-rated Rolls-Royce R-type.

This was a liquid-cooled, in-line V12 engine with a swept volume of some 37 litres capacity. With its ancestor having been developed for high-speed flight, the engine was relatively small in frontal area, considering its large internal capacity; this was a major factor in its favour, as the design criteria for the Griffon dictated that its overall dimensions be close to those of the Merlin, for reasons of interchangeability.

A major departure from the Merlin, and imposed as an Air Ministry design directive for all new aero-engines, rotation of the Griffon was in the opposite direction. This had a similar opposite effect on the combined torque-reaction and aerodynamic forces that caused an aircraft to veer towards one side of the runway during take-off; the tendency for the aircraft to swing now took place in the opposite direction, often catching out those pilots who were more used to Merlin-engined Spitfires. The Merlin-powered Spitfire tended to swing to the left during the take-off run, whereas Griffon-engined examples swung to the right. Early examples of the Griffon were somewhat less refined compared to its sibling and, reportedly, less smooth than the Merlin. Its larger engine capacity, and a different cylinder firing-order than that of the Merlin, endowed the Griffon with a much deeper and harsher-sounding exhaust note that soon earned it the epithet, "The Growler".

Griffon development was less spectacular than that of the Merlin in respect of the gain in overall power output achieved over that of the first production examples. In the summer of 1940, the Griffon II was rated at 1,720hp at sea level, and 1,495hp at 14,500ft. The Griffon VI that was fitted in the Spitfire Mark XII produced 1,815hp. However,

it still produced a substantial increase in rated power, especially with the advent, in 1943, of the Griffon 60-series, fitted with two-speed, two stage supercharging. The Griffon 65 produced 2,035hp at 7,000ft; the similar Griffon 66 drove a blower for cabin pressurisation in the Spitfire PRXIX.

Further advances in engine output were made in the Griffon 72 and 74 variants used in the Fairey Firefly, where the power at 9,250ft had risen to 2,245hp. Another major change was made in the Griffon 83 to 88 versions, which incorporated reduction gear units that drove contra-rotating propellers. The Griffon 101 featured a three-speed supercharger unit and was installed in a Spiteful aircraft that reached a speed of 494mph; this combination of engine and airframe suffered many problems during its testing programme and, therefore, did not go into production.

The cessation of hostilities did not bring an end to the Griffon as an operational engine: in addition to it remaining in service, well into the fifties in the later marks of the Spitfire, notably the PRXIX, the Griffon was selected to power the Avro Shackleton four-engined maritime reconnaissance aircraft. Its Griffon 57 and 57A engines were each fitted with dual three-bladed contra-rotating propellers and delivered 2,455hp at low-level. A water/methanol injection system was used to augment engine performance during take-off, particularly in hot climates and when heavily laden. The Griffon remained in front-line service until the retirement of the Shackleton in 1991.

MAIN
A Griffon 58
engine generally
used in Shackletons.

Chapter Five
From the Cockpit

*"Once you've flown a Spitfire, it spoils
you for all other fighters. Every other
aircraft seems imperfect in one way
or another." – Lt Colonel William
R Dunn, USAAF, ex-no 71
(Eagle) Squadron, Royal Air Force*

From the Cockpit

The Spitfire has been described as being "what every well-dressed fighter pilot wore." Almost universally accepted as being a magnificent fighting machine, it was not always the fastest fighter around, but its handling and overall reliability endeared it to those who flew it. Part of its success was due to the fact that every production Spitfire was thoroughly flight tested before being ferried to its operational unit. In 1938, the Vickers-Supermarine company's chief test pilot, Jeffrey Quill, devised the standardised test procedures that, with variations for different marks and engines, were used in testing all development and production Spitfires. Quill headed a team of around 10 or 12 pilots who jointly tested all of the Spitfires built at the Southampton factory. At the Castle Bromwich facility near Birmingham, from 1940 onwards, a team of some 25 pilots carried out the testing of all Spitfires produced at that site. Their chief test pilot, Alex Henshaw, personally carried out the production test flight on a total of some 2,360 Spitfires and Seafires between 1940 and 1946.

The production test flight was not a particularly lengthy process although, from Alex Henshaw's writings, it was a thorough test of the new aircraft's handling and performance. After some initial circuit work of around 10 minutes duration, where the general handling of the aircraft was carried out, in particular that of the trim system which could be adjusted to enable the aircraft to be flown "hands-off", the remainder of the test flight lasted around 20 to 30 minutes. This involved checking the aircraft's climb performance and the rated power output of the engine, calibrated against barometric pressure and temperature graphs. This was followed by a full-power dive in which the trim was set to give "hands and feet-off"

MAIN
The cockpit of a Spitfire Mark IX.

MAIN
The cockpit of a Spitfire Mark IX showing the undercarriage (Chassis) lever on the right.

From the Cockpit

stability at speeds of up to 460mph indicated air speed. Henshaw, personally, also performed some aerobatics to determine how good, or bad, that particular aircraft was. It is likely that the other test pilots did similarly, as few pilots would let such an opportunity pass them by!

Henshaw also wrote that earlier marks of Spitfire were much sprightlier handling aircraft than the later more powerful but heavier variants. His testing of the aircraft's roll-rate involved putting the aircraft into a flick-roll to see how many times it rolled; the Mark II and Mark V performed two and a half rolls, the heavier Mark IX gave only one and a half, while later variants failed to reach even that lower figure. Numerous incidents befell Alex during his long and potentially dangerous test career, including a spate of engine failures related to the skew drive gear in the Merlin engine, of which Henshaw himself suffered 11 out of 14 incidents! Emergency landings were interspersed with the odd crash or two. One of the more serious accidents happened following an engine failure at 800ft, close to Willenhall, near Wolverhampton. In an attempt to avoid a populated area, Henshaw tried to land in a cultivated area and clipped a tree that tore off one wing: the aircraft then hit a house which caused the engine and propeller, and the other wing, to be ripped off. The fuselage finally struck a concrete post and broke in half, leaving the somewhat relieved Alex alive, and able to fly many more Spitfires. On one occasion, on the orders of a higher authority, he carried out a roll manoeuvre while flying above Broad Street, in Birmingham, at a height, according to Henshaw of "around 50 feet."

Getting into the cockpit was no easy task for a Spitfire pilot, especially during the rush of an

MAIN
An RAF pilot climbing aboard a Spitfire.

MAIN
A squadron of Spitfires taking off.

From the Cockpit

MAIN
A pilot at the controls of a Spitfire.

operational "scramble". After first clambering onto the wing, it was then necessary to step over the sill of the hinged cockpit access door and stand on the pilot's seat cushion, before lowering the body into the sitting position. The word "cushion" is somewhat of a misnomer, as it did little to afford comfort. The seat pan contained the parachute with a dinghy pack on top of it; the latter's pressurised CO_2 inflation cylinder was a prominent feature, being in close contact with the rear end of the unfortunate flyer. Bearing in mind there was no actual cockpit floor, it was better to slide down into position and place the feet directly onto the rudder pedals. The absence of a floor also made things difficult, for pilots and ground crew alike, in the event of an object being dropped into the cockpit. Once installed in the cockpit, the pilot strapped into his parachute harness, connected the lanyard of the dinghy to toggles on his Mae West life-jacket, and tightly secured his seat harness.

Getting out in an emergency situation, given the relatively tight fit, was not an easy process either! In a combat situation with smoke and flames around the cockpit, coupled with g-forces and the possibility of pilot incapacity, it often needed almost superhuman qualities to escape the confines. Added to all that, the canopy first needed to be jettisoned. In all of its many marks and variations, the Spitfire's canopy offered its own contribution to the difficulty in exiting the pilot's workplace. The recognised procedure for jettisoning the canopy involved the pilot in first lowering his seat to its fullest extent. After undoing his seat harness, he then lowered his head as far as humanly possible, at the same time reaching up to grasp the release knob which, when pulled, acted upon a cable that disengaged the latching pins

From the Cockpit

from the canopy guide rails. Then, using his elbows, the pilot pushed the canopy off the rails. With good fortune, the canopy separated cleanly from the aircraft, allowing the pilot to abandon his aircraft, hopefully, without causing him any further harm. Shorter pilots drew some comfort from their lack of stature should a possible "bail-out" scenario arise.

Throughout the evolution of the Spitfire, there was a steady increase in the many levers and controls that were added around the already limited confines of the cockpit.

In addition to the original engine controls, trim wheels, undercarriage and flap levers, there were drop tank and bomb-releases, tailwheel locking (on some later marks) and,

From the Cockpit

for the naval versions, the arrestor hook and wing-folding controls. Pilots wore leather gloves for some protection from the cold, and also to reduce the possibility of laceration or grazing that could be received from contact with the often sharp edges of the controls themselves, or by their close proximity to other items of cockpit furnishings or aircraft structure. A small crow-bar, clipped to the drop-down cockpit access door, was fitted for use in an emergency situation.

The forward view from the cockpit was obscured while on the ground by the long nose that, due to the tailwheel configuration, pointed upwards from the horizontal. For the pilot to see ahead during taxying, it was necessary for him to weave the aircraft from side to side in a zigzag manner. It was not until the tail lifted during take-off that direct forward vision, over the nose, became possible. The nose also impeded the forward view during the landing phase of flight, leading to the adoption of the Spitfire's classic, curved final-approach to land. Once in the air, the pilot soon discovered the Spitfire's legendary handling qualities. According to Douglas Bader, "this was an aircraft par excellence, with its light, positive and well-harmonised controls." Its wide speed range, from a maximum of 367mph to a landing speed of around 60 to 65mph, was almost without equal.

Due to the less than ergonomic layout of the cockpit, when compared to that of a more modern aircraft, the pilot's movements in the take-off phase of flight, resembled those of an organist, as he moved both feet on the rudder pedals to keep the aircraft straight while, at the same time, changing hands on the grip of the control column in order to perform some

of his cockpit duties. Even from a ground observer's standpoint, it was fairly easy to tell the experience, on type, of a Spitfire pilot by the way the aircraft behaved on take-off.

When flown by a relative novice, it would sometimes lurch in a seemingly uncontrolled manner just after becoming airborne, as the pilot transferred his grasp of the spade-handled control column from his right hand to his left, in order to raise the undercarriage. This "change hands" procedure was brought about by the less than ideal placement of some of the key controls. The engine throttle, mixture, and propeller controls were on the left cockpit wall, and the undercarriage lever on the right. Further embarrassment could follow if the pilot had not applied sufficient friction adjustment to the throttle; a combination of engine vibration, and a bumpy airfield, could result in the throttle moving away from the take-off setting and thus reducing power during the critical period, albeit a short one, while he was raising the undercarriage.

During the take-off run, the aircraft was initially kept straight by small rudder adjustments that provided differential braking as the hand-operated brake lever, located on the spade-grip of the control column, was gently squeezed; as the air speed increased, the rudder became effective for maintaining directional control. Shortly after take-off, and on completion of the undercarriage-raising "organ recital", the pilot's hands then resumed their original tasks, after first giving a short squeeze of the brake lever to stop wheel rotation before the undercarriage entered its close-fitting housing. Once safely airborne, the engine throttle next required an intentional reduction in power to the 'climb' boost-setting, and the aircraft's trim controls that were also located on the left side of the cockpit, likewise needed some adjustment.

Merlin-powered Spitfires were considered to be much smoother when compared to their Griffon-engined relatives. Although they rotated in opposite directions, with a consequent opposite effect on torque and gyroscopic forces, both versions had one thing in common – power in abundance! An American pilot, Jeff Ethell, sadly no longer with us, described the feeling of flying a Griffon-powered Spitfire as being "... similar to that of driving a hot rod car, the feeling of unbridled horsepower being transmitted to the pilot through the seat of his pants." On later marks, the overall throttle lever movement was around four inches, effectively giving over 400hp for each inch of movement. Although Douglas Bader had described the controls of early marks of Spitfire as being well-harmonised, later versions were reportedly much less so: the elevator controls remained light and required a delicate touch in order that smooth changes in the pitch axis could be made; the rudder was relatively stiff in deflection, particularly at higher speeds, as were the ailerons, which needed a strong hand.

When landing, the Spitfire was characterised by its curved final approach path to the runway, necessary because of the limited forward view from the cockpit. In most other respects, landing was not overly dramatic, bearing in mind its narrow-tracked undercarriage. With docile handling down to a very slow speed its sometimes inexperienced pilot was usually able to make a decent three-point touchdown. Inevitably, there were occasional mishaps during the return to terra firma, some resulting from undercarriage malfunction or battle

damage, or as a result of over-enthusiastic use of the brakes during the landing run, which caused the aircraft to nose-over.

The handling characteristics, especially those of some later variants would, at first, appear to be contrary to the requirements for aerial combat. However, coupled with the aerodynamics bestowed on it by Mitchell's design team, the intensive flight testing programme of the airframe and engine, and the skill and courage of those who flew it, the Spitfire achieved its deserved, legendary status as a fighting machine. Its capability of performing, and maintaining, a very tight turning radius often gained its pilot the upper hand over an adversary. The Mark I, with its eight Browning 0.303in machine guns or, four machine guns and two 20mm cannon, was the version of the Spitfire that, together with the Hurricane, formed the mainstay of RAF Fighter Command at the outbreak of WW2.

At the commencement of hostilities in 1939, orders had been placed for a total of 2,143 Spitfires. The first RAF unit, No 19 Squadron at Duxford, had received its first 1,030hp Merlin II-engined, Mark I aircraft between August and December 1938 and, by the following September, a further nine squadrons were similarly equipped. Deliveries of the Mark II, with the more powerful Merlin XII of 1,175hp, began in June 1940, although it did not appear in large numbers until much later in that year. By the early part of July 1940, 19 squadrons of Spitfires were operational. It was mainly the Mark I, together with the more numerous Hurricane, that carried out the task of defending Britain from the air in those critical days of war.

MAIN
A Spitfire of No 72
Squadron on patrol.

Chapter Six

Like a Duck to Water

Like a Duck to Water

Supermarine Spitfire float-planes. When the Germans invaded Norway in April 1940, there arose an urgent requirement for a float-plane fighter aircraft that could operate from the Norwegian Fjords in the, as yet, unoccupied parts of that territory. Due to the difficult terrain of the region, and the lack of airfields or other ground that would be suitable for aircraft operations outside of the enemy-occupied areas, the only option was for a water-based fighter.

The task was given to the Vickers-Supermarine company who had a wealth of experience in high-speed, water-borne flight; their Schneider Trophy-winning experience could be vital to the successful and prompt completion of a suitable aircraft. Its ancestry made the Spitfire a prime candidate for conversion to a float-plane configuration. A Mark I Spitfire was selected for modifications at the Woolston factory. Due to the urgency of the military situation in Norway, there was insufficient time to design, build, and test a set of floats for the Spitfire from first principles; therefore, a set of floats from the Fleet Air Arm fighter, the Blackburn Roc, were used as a starting point for the conversion.

Tests, using a one-seventh scale model, were carried out in the hydrodynamics test tank facility at Farnborough, where the Supermarine company had tested their S6-series of aircraft. The results were promising, although the vertical tail surfaces needed to be increased to counter the effects of the large side areas of the two floats. Accordingly, a ventral fin was added, in place of the now redundant tailwheel. However, the military situation in Norway soon deteriorated, ending in withdrawal by the Allies, so the float-plane Spitfire project, informally known as the Narvik Nightmare, was cancelled.

MAIN
A Spitfire fighter
is lowered into
the hangar of an
aircraft carrier, as
another plane waits
to take off in the
background.

RIGHT
A Griffon-
powered Seafire
XVII with wings
and tips folded.

With the ventral fin and floats removed, and its tailwheel assembly refitted, the aircraft was converted back to its original fighter role.

Early 1942 saw the revival of the float-plane fighter project, this time for use in the eastern Mediterranean and Aegean, following the German invasion of the Greek islands. The objective was to disrupt the supply chain to the occupying forces that relied heavily on air transport; a float-plane fighter was seen as one possible option, operating from sheltered waters in that region, and relying on the British bases in Egypt for its own support needs. Resulting from the promise shown in the earlier float-plane project, the Spitfire was again selected for conversion, this time a Mark V. Powered by a Merlin 45 driving a four-bladed propeller, this aircraft was fitted with two floats, a ventral fin extension in place of the tailwheel, and a Vokes-type air filter was added to the carburettor intake under the engine. Additionally, four strong lifting-points were fitted, two forward of the cockpit, and the other two behind, for hoisting the complete aircraft from the water during transfer to a ship or shore facility. For flight testing, the aircraft was fitted with a spin-recovery parachute, the location of which required the installation of a protective guard in front of the rudder horn balance to prevent the parachute line from fouling the rudder. Fortunately, the spin-recovery system was not called upon.

The Mark V float-plane made its first flight on 12 October 1942, flown by Jeffrey Quill. Aside from the change from the Vokes to an Aero-Vee filter, and an extension forwards of the engine intake duct to prevent the ingestion of spray, there were few modifications made. Armed to the Mark VB standard, this aircraft, and a further two that had been converted by

MAIN
Spitfires banking in shafts of sunlight.

the Folland Aircraft Company, arrived by sea in Egypt in October 1943. By the time of their arrival, the original requirement for float-plane fighters had been overtaken by events, particularly the loss of the islands of Kos and Leros to enemy forces: the aircraft were instead sent to operate from the Great Bitter Lake on the Suez Canal. Despite the encumbrance of their float gear, the Spitfire VB float-planes were still quite reasonable performers, with a top speed of 324mph at 19,500ft, a service ceiling of 33,000ft, and a maximum climb rate of 2,450ft/min at 15,500ft.

The war in the Pacific theatre was also seen as an area of operations in which a float-plane fighter could serve a useful purpose, especially around the many islands. This time, a Spitfire Mark IX was

the basis for conversion which, on completion, gave it a broadly similar external appearance to its water-borne Mark V predecessors. Again, the project did not reach fruition as the float-plane fighter concept was abandoned, the only Mark IX that had been fitted with floats being converted back to a land-based fighter. Its test pilot, Jeffrey Quill, wrote in his appraisal of its qualities: "The Spitfire IX on floats was faster than the standard Hurricane. Its handling on the water was extremely good and its only unusual feature was a tendency to 'tramp' from side to side on the floats, or to 'waddle' a bit when at high speed in the plane" – the reference to "the plane" being the point at which its speed over the water caused the aircraft to rise onto the stepped portion of the floats.

MAIN Supermarine Rolls Royce Seaplane, S6B S1595, 1931. This plane was designed by Reginald G Mitchell (1895-1937), the designer of several world-beating seaplanes and the famous Supermarine Spitfire.

Like a Duck to Water

At the outbreak of war in 1939, carrier-based Fleet defence was the province of such ageing aircraft designs as the Gloster Sea Gladiator; this was shortly to be supplemented in 1940 by the Fairey Fulmar, a development of the land-based Fairey Battle light bomber. At the time, it was Royal Navy policy that all of its carrier-borne aircraft should carry a navigator: this had imposed a design requirement for a minimum of two crew-members to be carried that resulted in the Fulmar being too heavy. Its weight reduced its climb performance and, therefore, imposed a consequent reduction in its ability to engage with enemy fighters. The Fairey Firefly was powered by a 1,730hp Griffon, instead of the Merlin of the Fulmar, and with the greater fire-power of four 20mm cannon over the Fulmar's eight machine guns, was not destined to reach carrier squadrons until late in 1943. The two-crew stipulation was later removed, opening the way for the introduction of single-seat fighter aircraft into the Fleet Air Arm.

Some American lend-lease carrier aircraft were drafted into service, to help fill the shortfall, namely the Grumman Martlet, as was the introduction of the British-built Hawker Sea Hurricane, a conversion of the ageing land-based fighter. The adaptability and inherent reliability of the Spitfire, in addition to its excellent performance and air combat qualities, was soon to see it take on a different role than that for which it was originally intended. Few could ever have envisaged, during its design and early development, that there was even the slightest possibility of this aircraft being utilised in a maritime role.

Supermarine Seafire (officially named Sea Spitfire). This was a naval version of the Spitfire and became the first modern,

Like a Duck to Water

At the outbreak of war in 1939, carrier-based Fleet defence was the province of such ageing aircraft designs as the Gloster Sea Gladiator; this was shortly to be supplemented in 1940 by the Fairey Fulmar, a development of the land-based Fairey Battle light bomber. At the time, it was Royal Navy policy that all of its carrier-borne aircraft should carry a navigator: this had imposed a design requirement for a minimum of two crew-members to be carried that resulted in the Fulmar being too heavy. Its weight reduced its climb performance and, therefore, imposed a consequent reduction in its ability to engage with enemy fighters. The Fairey Firefly was powered by a 1,730hp Griffon, instead of the Merlin of the Fulmar, and with the greater fire-power of four 20mm cannon over the Fulmar's eight machine guns, was not destined to reach carrier squadrons until late in 1943. The two-crew stipulation was later removed, opening the way for the introduction of single-seat fighter aircraft into the Fleet Air Arm.

Some American lend-lease carrier aircraft were drafted into service, to help fill the shortfall, namely the Grumman Martlet, as was the introduction of the British-built Hawker Sea Hurricane, a conversion of the ageing land-based fighter. The adaptability and inherent reliability of the Spitfire, in addition to its excellent performance and air combat qualities, was soon to see it take on a different role than that for which it was originally intended. Few could ever have envisaged, during its design and early development, that there was even the slightest possibility of this aircraft being utilised in a maritime role.

Supermarine Seafire (officially named Sea Spitfire). This was a naval version of the Spitfire and became the first modern, carrier-based fighter to join the inventory of the Royal Navy. Principally intended for use on aircraft carriers, the Seafire was endowed with equipment necessary for operations on that type of vessel, including a tail hook, strong-points for catapult attachment, and on later variants, wing-folding arrangements. In its earliest form, the Seafire was less than ideal for carrier-borne operations, particularly because of its narrow-track undercarriage, but some of the disadvantages were outweighed by its performance as a fast, rapid-climbing fleet defence fighter.

Type 340–Seafire Mark IB. Even before the outbreak of war, the Admiralty had, in 1938, made an approach to the Air Ministry for a naval version of the Spitfire but their approaches were turned down, as were a further two requests in early 1940. The following year, the Royal Navy (RN) was offered some modified Spitfire Mark I land-planes to fill their urgent combat fighter needs, although their Lordships at the Admiralty had demanded they be given the latest Mark V version. Their wishes were fulfilled when, in September 1941, the Admiralty was allowed to place an order for 250 Spitfire Mark VA and VB aircraft, even though they had not yet finalised the list of modifications that were necessary for carrier operations. To assist in training of the RN pilots, the RAF loaned a large number of Mark VA and VBs, the majority having first been fitted with tail hooks.

In service, the main drawback in operating the Seafire I was its relative fragility, as it had been designed without the much greater stresses imposed by carrier operations being taken into account. The limited forward visibility from the cockpit during the approach to the flight deck made life especially difficult for the pilot,

MAIN
A restored
Supermarine
Mark IX Spitfire.

MAIN
A beautifully
restored example
of a Seafire XVII.

as the carrier was often moving vertically, as well as forwards, during this critical phase of flight. In the subsequent landing, often a very heavy one when compared with a typical airfield arrival, an undercarriage collapse was commonplace, as was damage caused to the rear fuselage structure by the rebound of the tail

hook from the deck, following a failed attempt to trap the arrestor wire. It has been claimed that more Seafire I aircraft were lost in landing accidents than those due to enemy action.

Type 357–Seafire Mark IIC. The specifically-modified "naval" version of the Mark V was known as the Seafire II. This

mark featured a substantial strengthening of the airframe in critical areas, provision of hard points for the carriage of under-wing stores, and a major redesign of the main undercarriage; this was lengthened, and raked forward, to improve both its landing characteristics, and its general deck handling capabilities. Unfortunately, little could be done about improving the forward view. Notwithstanding its drawbacks, the Seafire was a welcome addition to the carrier force, bringing its known outstanding capabilities as an interceptor fighter to its new role as a fleet defender. Somewhat heavier than the land-based aircraft it was based on, it was a great improvement over the previous fleet defence

aircraft such as the Sea Gladiator, although the by now ageing Sea Hurricane fighter did sterling work in similar circumstances. As for the Seafire, the Sea Hurricane had been converted from a land-based fighter.

Type 358-Seafire Mark III. In 1943, the Seafire Mark III entered service and was the first Seafire to have a manually-operated foldable wing for below-deck storage. After the first batch of Mark IIIs, later LF Mark IIIs that were optimised for low-level operations, and fitted with the Merlin 55M engine, formed the bulk of over 1,000 produced. Some of the earlier Mark II and III fighters were each fitted with two F24 cameras and

MAIN
An RAF salvage unit try
to manoeuvre a Seafire
IIC in a sea of mud
during WW2.

used in the maritime fighter reconnaissance role, in which they proved highly successful.

Type 337–Seafire Mark XV. This version's out-of-sequence numbering resulted from an attempt at rationalising the numbering across the various marks of Spitfire and Seafire. The Mark XV was the sea-going equivalent of the Spitfire XII with two symmetrical under-wing radiators, a 1,750hp Griffon VI driving a four-bladed propeller and broader-chord rudder. One obvious difference was the retractable tailwheel and arrestor hook.

Type 395–Seafire Mark XVII. The last batch of Mark XVs built were modified to become the Mark XVII, and had a cut-down rear fuselage, a curved windscreen, bubble canopy, and wing fuel tanks. It also featured a strengthened undercarriage, and a larger area fin and rudder. As the Spitfire numbering was changed from Roman to Arabic numerals around this time, so was that of the Seafire, their marks being numbered from 40 onwards; the Mark XVII is also, somewhat confusingly, known as the Mark 41.

Type 388–Seafire 45. The navalised equivalent of the Spitfire Mark 21, with the new wing and Griffon 61 engine. In a short production run, only 50 were built.

Type 388–Seafire 46. First Seafire to have the dual three-bladed contra-rotating propeller, that effectively eliminated the torque swing on take-off, fitted as standard. The absence of wing-folding contributed to the relatively short production run of only 24 examples. Originally part of the Admiralty's Spitfire Mark V order placement, this order was transferred to an order for the Spitfire 21 before eventually being designated as the Seafire 46.

Type 388–Seafire 47. Probably the best of
the Seafires, this mark had a 2,200hp Griffon
driving a contra-rotating propeller, and the
enlarged tailplane and fin/rudder assembly
from the Spiteful. A total of 90 were built.

Type 383–Seafang. The navalised version of
the Spiteful, the first examples, designated Seafang
F31, being based on a conversion from a Spiteful
XV. Only nine were built. The Seafang F32 had
a larger fuel capacity, and featured folding wing
tips, a 2,350hp Griffon 89 or 90 driving a new
Rotol-designed, dual three-bladed contra-rotating
propeller. Armed with four 20mm cannon, it
had provision for carrying two 1,000lb bombs
or four 60lb rockets. With a service ceiling of
41,000ft, its initial climb rate was a more than
respectable 4,630ft/min. Only two reached final
assembly from a batch of 10 sets of parts made.

Although it was very fast, the Seafang, having
been derived from the Spiteful, the fastest
propeller-driven piston-engined aircraft ever
built in Britain with a top speed of 494mph,
was not particularly good at low speeds.
Its performance did not offer much of an
improvement over that of the excellent Seafire
47, so the Fleet Air Arm selected the Hawker
Sea Fury for the fleet fighter role instead.

The Seafire in its various guises also attracted
attention from Commonwealth and foreign
naval air services, and was even tested in the
USA as a potential choice for the US Navy
ship-borne fighter; however, no order was
forthcoming. Thirty-five Seafires saw service
with the Royal Canadian Navy between 1946
and 1954, operating from the carrier HMCS
Warrior and naval shore bases. The RN
Fleet Air Arm operated Seafires on front-line
duties until 1951, and the type remained in
service with the RNVR until late in 1954.

MAIN
A cannon-armed
Seafire on the
deck of HMS
Indomitable.

Chapter Seven
Eyes in the Skies

Eyes in the Skies

Britain was not fully prepared for the outbreak of the war in 1939, both in its shortage of modern fighters and bombers, and its lack of suitable reconnaissance aircraft. Originally, it was planned to use the Bristol Blenheim bomber in the long-range reconnaissance role, and the Westland Lysander for shorter ranges. At the start of the war, photographic reconnaissance was carried out mostly by operational squadrons on an ad hoc basis. A Blenheim carried out the first operational RAF sortie of the war when a Mark IV of No 139 Squadron flew a photo reconnaissance mission over German naval forces, near the German coast, on the first day of the conflict on 3 September 1939.

Both of these aircraft types were susceptible to attack from the air by enemy fighters; they were also extremely vulnerable to ground or ship-based anti-aircraft fire. During the early part of the war in France and Belgium, the Lysander had proved no match for the enemy due largely to its slow speed, lack of defensive armament, and poor agility. Of the 174 Lysanders sent to France, 88 were lost in the air, and a further 30 were destroyed on the ground. Clearly, Britain needed a much more suitable alternative; this had been recognised, and even suggested, prior to the outbreak of war. The concept of a fast monoplane, optimised for photographic reconnaissance duties; began to be realised in October 1939, when two Mark I Spitfires were selected for conversion.

Shortly before the onset of war, an Australian-born RAF veteran of WW1, Sidney Cotton, had been recruited by the British intelligence services. Cotton, whose business and social activities could be described as less than conventional, had a wealth of flying experience, including high-altitude flight and aerial photography. In the period leading up to the commencement of hostilities, Cotton had carried out a number of covert photographic missions under the guise of business trips that took him near to, and sometimes overhead, German military installations and other strategic industrial locations in his Lockheed Electra Junior. This aircraft had been financed by the British intelligence services, and was fitted with three concealed F24 cameras, operated by a hidden control under the pilot's seat: Cotton had actually taken photographs of German installations, undetected, while carrying a senior Luftwaffe officer, Albert Kesselring, on a "joy-ride" over Berlin. The Electra was claimed to have been the last civilian aircraft to leave that city prior to the outbreak of WW2.

With his already vast experience, in both high-altitude aviation and aerial photography, Cotton was a good choice to head the new RAF No 1 Photographic Development Unit (PDU) at Heston, later to become No 1 Photographic Reconnaissance Unit (PRU) based at Hendon. Initially designated as No 2 Camouflage Unit, the unit's somewhat ironical naming was intended to deflect unwanted attention from its real activities, the new unit began its task of improving the RAF's rather poor reconnaissance capability. This it did to great effect: by the end of the war, RAF reconnaissance had improved beyond all expectations, due mainly to the efforts of No 1 PDU. After perfecting techniques in the more traditional methods of aerial photography of ground targets, from aircraft operating at great altitudes and high speeds, their pioneering use of both oblique and stereoscopic photography was fundamental, later in the war, in countering the threat of the German V1 and V2 weapons. These new photographic

MAIN
The Blenheim Mark IV carried out the first operational RAF sortie of the war on a photo reconnaissance mission.

MAIN
A Spitfire Mark XI
with split pair
camera ports under
the fuselage, aft of
the wing roots.

MAIN
Spitfire Mark IIC serial
P7350 is the oldest
airworthy example in
the world and the only
Spitfire still flying today
to have actually fought in
the Battle of Britain.

MAIN
A 1942 Supermarine
Spitfire Mark IX.

techniques revealed the exact locations of the characteristic V1 launching ramps, and many of the V2 launching and storage sites. Cotton also had his aircraft painted in a light blue finish, similar to that of his Electra, a colour that made the, mostly unarmed, reconnaissance aircraft difficult to see while in flight.

At the outset, Cotton's unit operated the Blenheim, which he claimed was too slow, but he successfully lobbied higher authority for his unit to be given the Spitfire. The first two aircraft allocated to the unit were to be the precursors of around 1,000 Spitfires that were either converted, or built specifically, for the Photographic Reconnaissance (PR) role. Although much less in the public domain than their much-lauded fighter cousins, for reasons of military necessity in wartime, their contribution to British and Allied operations was significant; regrettably, the reconnaissance Spitfires, and the men that flew them, did not achieve the widespread recognition their exploits deserved.

There were many developments of the reconnaissance Spitfire; as had happened with the fighter, these aircraft inherited a similarly bewildering method of numbering types and variants. Until late 1941, Spitfire PR types were identified by letters, the six versions produced prior to that time having been allocated the letters A to F. This led to some confusion with the Spitfire wing types which bore similar letter designations. From the autumn of 1941, letters were replaced by Roman numerals, the six types that had been previously identified by letters now becoming PR Marks I to VI, although the first two had largely been superseded by this time. However, the new identifiers brought still further confusion to the Spitfire story, as the Spitfire Mark VII fighter, and the PR

MAIN
Spitfire Mark XI
which was used in
high-speed diving
trials in 1944.

Mark VII, are substantially different aircraft: the fighter Mark VII had a Merlin 60 or 70-series engine and a B-type wing, with two 20mm cannon and four 0.303in machine guns; the PR Mark VII had a Merlin 45 engine, a large oil tank under the nose and, being based on the Spitfire IA, had an eight machine-gun wing, plus an extra fuel tank in the rear fuselage. From the PR Mark X onwards, discrete numbers were allocated to either the fighter version or the PR version, thereby simplifying things somewhat, although there was a further fly in the Spitfire ointment. The introduction of an occasional Fighter Reconnaissance (FR) version, some of which bore a combination of Roman numerals and a letter suffix, e.g. the Spitfire FR Mark XIVe, added to the already chaotic Spitfire mark identification system.

The early PRs were, in essence, fairly straightforward adaptations of the Spitfire Mark IA. Guns were removed to reduce weight, and their ports faired over. Joints between various parts of the aircraft structure, access panel gaps, and the like, were closed over to reduce drag and, therefore, increase speed. With the addition of cameras, this was a reasonable starting point for what was eventually to become a highly-optimised and successful photographic reconnaissance aircraft. Together with the de Havilland Mosquito PR aircraft, it was a valuable asset in both the air and ground offensives against enemy forces, and strategic targets, in mainland Europe, North Africa, and other campaigns east of Suez.

PR Type A (PR Mark I). With its guns removed and their ports faired over, this mark had an improved-visibility cockpit canopy that featured a large transparent perspex blister on each side. A downward-facing F24

MAIN
Photograph of the breached Möhne Dam taken from a Spitfire PR IX.

camera was installed in the inner gun bay of each wing. One of this type became the first Spitfire to operate overseas when it joined British Expeditionary Forces (BEF) in France, in November 1939, flying its first mission that was aborted due to cloud cover over Aachen, on 18 November. Both aircraft were later converted to PR Mark III standard.

PR Type B (PR Mark II). Improvements over the PR Mark I included the addition of an extra 29-gallon fuel tank behind the cockpit, and the F24 camera was upgraded from a 5in to an 8in focal-length lens. The PR Mark II was first used on 10 February 1940, when this aircraft successfully photographed the German naval bases at Emden and Wilhelmshaven.

PR Type C (PR Mark III). Entered service in March 1940. The first PR to be produced in numbers; a total of 40 were produced by converting existing marks of Spitfire fighters. Extended range was endowed by the 30-gallon capacity fuel tank that was fitted under the port wing; a blister under the starboard wing housed two F24 cameras with 8in lenses. Provision was also made for an additional F24 camera to be vertically-mounted in the rear fuselage.

PR Type D (PR Mark IV). Nicknamed "the bowser", its 114 gallons of fuel made it capable of reaching Stettin, on the Baltic coast of Germany; at 2,000 miles, its range was the greatest of all early Spitfires. Entering service in October 1940, a total of 229 aircraft were produced. Each PR Mark IV was given a letter code relating to the complement of camera(s) carried: W – two F8 with 20in lenses; X – one F24 with a 14in lens; Y – one F52 with a 36in lens; S – two F24 with 14in lenses.

PR Type E (PR Mark V). Only one of this mark was produced but it blazed the trail for others to be fitted with a similar obliquely-mounted camera; this development gave the Spitfire the ability to carry out low-level photography at 90° to the direction of travel, thus eliminating the need for direct overflight of the target and thus reduced the risk of being hit by enemy defensive fire.

PR Type F (PR Mark VI). This was an interim, out-of-sequence design that was produced prior to the appearance of the PR Mark IV; the first of the 15 built entered service in March 1940. It had two under-wing fuel tanks, each holding 30 gallons, and an additional fuselage tank that together gave the aircraft sufficient endurance for a round trip to Berlin of up to four and a half hours duration. The first Berlin flight was made on 14 March 1941 with two F24 cameras with 8in lenses, later replaced by two F8 cameras with 20in lenses. Some Mark VIs carried an oblique-mounted F24 with a 14in lens.

PR Mark VII. This was the first Spitfire PR variant to be fitted with armament, as the low-level role took it into areas that were patrolled by enemy fighters. Fitted with the eight machine guns from the fighter Mark IA, it also carried the extra-range fuselage tank; cameras were two vertically-mounted F24s, with 5in and 14in lenses respectively and an oblique F24 with a 14in lens. The oblique camera could be fitted so that it faced either port, or starboard. Production was 45 PR Mark VIIs, converted from Mark V fighters.

PR Mark IX. A short-term fix whereby a small number of Mark IX fighters were stripped of their armament and fitted with two vertically-mounted cameras.

FR Mark IX. Used for low-level and medium-level reconnaissance, these were the most heavily-armed of all the reconnaissance Spitfire marks. A true fighter reconnaissance aircraft, they all carried the standard gun arrangement of the Mark IX fighter, together with an oblique F24 camera.

PR Mark X. Another out-of-sequence variant that appeared in early 1944, almost a year after the Mark XI. Based on the Mark VII fighter fuselage, it had the wings of a Mark XI but with two 66-gallon fuel tanks in place of the guns. Withdrawn from service in September 1945, only 16 were produced.

PR Mark XI. Produced in greater numbers than any other PR variant with a total of over 470 having been built. It was based on a much modified PR Mark IX fuselage that had the extra fuselage fuel tank, as for that fitted on many PRs, and wing fuel tanks. Entering service in the summer of 1943, it was the first PR variant to be fitted with a "universal" camera installation that would allow rapid changes between the selection of cameras it could carry. These ranged from two F52 x 36in focal length, two F8 x 20in, one F52 x 20in and two F24 x 14in, with another F24 x 14in (or 8in) mounted obliquely. Some aircraft carried an additional F24 x 5in camera mounted behind a wheel-well for the low-to-medium altitude ranges of photographic work.

RIGHT
A Spitfire PR XIX with a Griffon engine driving two contra-rotating propellers.

PR Mark XIII. Entering service in late summer of 1942, the Mark XIII was an armed low-level reconnaissance fighter with a four-gun defensive armament. Although its range was somewhat limited by its gun installation, it proved invaluable in the preparations for the Normandy landings in 1944. It was converted from the Mark I and Mark V

MAIN
Spitfire P7350
"Enniskillen".

fighters, and the PR Mark VII. Cameras were three F24s, two vertical and one oblique.

PR Mark XIX. Built by combining the fuselage of the Mark XIV fighter with the pressurised cabin of the PR Mark X, this being incorporated into all, except for the first 22 examples, of the 225 that were built. The wings were those of the PR Mark X. The Mark XIX

MAIN
Spitfire PR XI,
serial PL965 was
built in 1944.

MAIN
A comparatively
rare Spitfire Tr 9
two-seater.

was the only Griffon-powered PR variant, and had an internal fuel capacity of up to 254 gallons. It was cleared to carry a drop tank with a further 170 gallons, although the largest used on operations held 70 gallons. The camera installation allowed for two vertical cameras and one oblique camera on the port side: vertical cameras were usually F8s with 14in or 20in focal length lenses or F52s with 20in lenses, the oblique camera was an F24 with either an 8in or 14in lens. The PR Mark XIX was the ultimate PR version: its top speed of 445mph,

and a service ceiling of 42,600ft, made it an almost impossible feat for a Luftwaffe fighter to catch it. Its first flight was in April 1944, becoming operational in the following month. Remaining in RAF service as an operational reconnaissance aircraft for one month short of

20 years, its swan-song took place on 1 April 1954. The PR XIX continued to fly for a further three years, three aircraft being used on meteorological duties with the Temperature and Humidity Flight, at RAF Woodvale, until their retirement on 10 June 1957.

MAIN
A clipped wing Spitfire XIV. Note the five-bladed propeller.

Force Aérienne

Chapter Eight

Spitfire
Notes
and
Anecdotes

Spitfire Notes and Anecdotes

There are around 50 Spitfires, and a small number of Seafires, still flying today. The actual number fluctuates from year to year, due to some of them undergoing heavy maintenance, partial restoration or, in extreme cases, a complete rebuild. The fact that so many are still capable of flight, over 70 years after the prototype K5054 first flew, is tribute to the dedicated and painstaking work of Spitfire enthusiasts the world over. In addition to those aircraft that are capable of flight, there are also a large number on static display in museums and private exhibitions. Such is the demand for a Spitfire to be put on display that many replicas have been produced. Had it not been such a successful and historic aircraft, this aircraft would still be in great demand: its classic lines have an aesthetic appeal that places the Spitfire firmly in the category – "If it looks right, it is right."

The Spitfire is known, and loved, by many who were yet to be born when this charismatic aircraft was both a symbol of hope, and defender of Britain, in the dark days of war. Spitfires can regularly be seen in flight at air shows. The RAF Battle of Britain Memorial Flight (BBMF) is in great demand for fly-pasts at ceremonial events and air displays, and can be seen regularly with one or more of its five airworthy Spitfires. A single Spitfire usually flies in a formation of three aircraft, together with a Hurricane and a Lancaster Bomber, paying tribute to the longevity of these amazing aircraft. As the name of the unit signifies, each flight that takes place is an airborne memorial to those who fought, and died, in the defence of their country in the great aerial conflicts of WW2. The appearance of the BBMF formation at an air show or other event is not only a visual delight; it is one of the few occasions that the evocative sound of

MAIN
Spitfire P7350 behind a Hawker Hurricane.

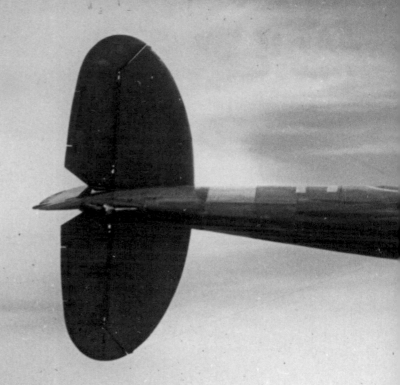

the Merlin engine, itself a memorable occasion, can be heard in its natural environment by aviation enthusiasts and the general public alike.

Delivered in August 1940, Spitfire Mark IIA serial number P7350 is the oldest airworthy example remaining, and is operated by the BBMF. It served with Nos 266, 603, 616 and 64 Squadrons of the RAF and later, with 57 OTU. In 1946 it was sold for scrap,

Spitfire Notes and Anecdotes

MAIN
Top scoring pilot Johnnie Johnson recreating a pose from a picture that was taken of him in 1944 in Normandy on the wing of a Spitfire.

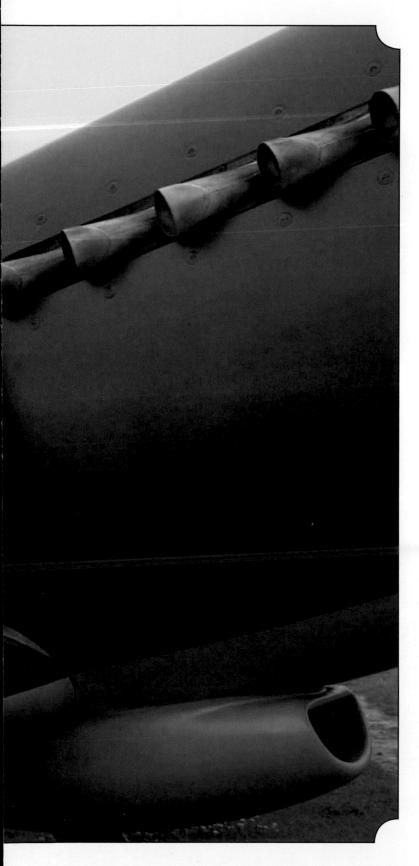

together with its aircraft log book, to John Dale & Sons: fortunately, they realised the importance of this aircraft, and it was reprieved, later being safely delivered to the RAF Colerne Museum. In 1967 it went into "make-up" in readiness for its starring role in the film The Battle of Britain: after filming had been completed, it was allocated to the BBMF where it has remained ever since.

The transition from the outmoded fighters, such as the Gloster Gladiator that were equipping front-line RAF squadrons at the start of WW2, onto the Spitfire, was not a particularly trouble-free exercise. Until then, fighter pilots had flown slower, open-cockpit aircraft with a fixed undercarriage: many found it difficult to adapt to the more modern newcomer, especially as it was a single-seater, with no trainer variant to ease the path to competence. The original canopy on the Spitfire Mark I had its top and sides flush with the line of the fuselage; the restricted headroom was particularly claustrophobic and made things difficult for taller pilots, many of whom, as a result, flew with the canopy open. The introduction of the bulged, Malcolm-type cockpit canopy gave a large increase in headroom while, at the same time, substantially improving the all-round visibility when airborne. While on the ground, nothing could be done that would greatly improve the pilot's forward visibility. The zigzag manoeuvre that typified the Spitfire while taxying was, in itself, responsible for the occasional, inadvertent "coming together" with another aircraft or item of ground equipment. The net result, for the hapless pilot involved, was to spend a few quaking moments in front of the CO's desk; for the maintenance crew, it was an unscheduled addition to their workload.

MAIN
Group Captain Douglas Bader sits in the cockpit of his Supermarine Spitfire, preparing with other pilots to take off for the "Battle of Britain Day" anniversary.

Spitfire Notes and Anecdotes

MAIN
Pilots of the Free
French Spitfire
Squadron running
to their planes.

Spitfire Notes and Anecdotes

The retractable undercarriage of the Spitfire was also unfamiliar to many pilots, and their failing to lower the undercarriage before landing was the cause of many landing accidents: further embarrassment was heaped upon the unfortunate flier when it was discovered that he had previously switched off the undercarriage warning klaxon, due to its often spurious operation caused by vibration or other mechanical action. A narrow-tracked undercarriage made cross-wind landings hazardous for the less-experienced, although the aircraft's good low-speed qualities were relatively forgiving in most other situations. A pronounced swing on take-off was another trap for the unwary, newly-converted Spitfire pilot who was hitherto not familiar with a combination of prodigious amounts of torque and the aerodynamic and gyroscopic forces involved; some more experienced pilots were also caught unawares. Coupled with the unergonomic cockpit layout, any (or all) of the foregoing possibilities conspired to provide the new pilot with an exciting time. Having gained the necessary experience on type, and mastered the art of flying, and fighting, in the Spitfire, most were totally captivated by it.

Probably one of the most famous Spitfires of the war was that flown by (then) Wing Commander J E (Johnnie) Johnson, a Mark IX, serial number EN398. In 1943, with his current tally of seven confirmed enemy aircraft destroyed and two shared "kills", four probables, and five damaged, Johnson was posted to RAF Kenley to lead a wing of four Canadian units: two squadrons flew the Spitfire Mark V, and two the Mark IX. Johnson had already flown the Mark V but soon chose the Mark IX as his personal aircraft. He quickly fell for his new

165

MAIN
A Spitfire LF Mark
IX with a name
dedication painted
on the side.

Spitfire Notes and Anecdotes

mount; after a test flight, he described her as "... very fast, the engine was sweet and she responded to the controls as only a thoroughbred can. I decided that she should be mine, and I never had occasion to regret the choice."

He had his initials painted on her as the squadron code "JE-J" and, instead of the usual "spread" pattern of gun harmonisation, had the aircraft's cannon and machine guns re-harmonised to converge at a single point in front of the aircraft. This was a mark of confidence in his own air gunnery skills as this left little margin for error, although his shots on target would be concentrated to deadly effect. Apart from a small idiosyncrasy of EN398, in that the aircraft that showed a permanent off-centre indication on the turn-and-bank gauge when in straight and level flight, both pilot and machine were as one, and Johnson flew her almost exclusively while in command of the Canadian wing. In six months of flying EN398, Johnson added another 12 "kills" and five others shared, with a further six damaged with one other shared. The aircraft's own tally of 15 and one-sixth enemy aircraft destroyed, and six and a half damaged, is even more remarkable as it never suffered damage from enemy fire, neither did it fail to complete a mission through technical malfunction.

Johnson's experience ranged across three marks of Spitfire: apart from the aforementioned Mark IX, he also flew the Mark VB and the XIVe. His total of 38 enemy aircraft destroyed made him the top scoring British pilot of the war, a total that was all the more creditable in that all of his victories were against fighter aircraft. The fate of his famous mount EN398 was rather ignominious for such a celebrated aircraft of her day; after

spending some of the wartime period being repaired after an accident while on charge with a Canadian squadron, followed by a lengthy period in storage, she became a training aircraft for French pilots in late 1954. After several post-war years in storage, EN398 was unceremoniously sold for scrap in October 1949.

There are many stories surrounding the history of the Spitfire, some tell of heroic deeds carried out in air combat, or during offensives against ground targets, while other tales recount events that covered the relatively mundane, day-to-day lives of RAF personnel during the wartime and subsequent operations. Occasionally, there occurred an event that even those involved would describe as being somewhat unusual, or even bizarre. The practice of carrying out the ground running of a newly installed engine, followed by an air test, is a routine that will be familiar to those with knowledge of RAF aircraft engineering procedures. A similar routine, in the form of an engine power check, takes place prior to every take-off. On most occasions, things go relatively smoothly: sometimes, things do not always go exactly according to plan, as was the case in one of these happenings that has become firmly embedded in Spitfire history.

Those present on Hibaldstow Airfield in Lincolnshire, a satellite of RAF Kirton-in-Lindsey, one day in early 1945, witnessed an event that had started out as commonplace, but subsequently unfolded in a remarkable sequence of events. The main characters were a pilot, Flt Lt Neil Cox DFC from No 53 OTU, Spitfire Mark VB serial number AB910, and a WAAF ground crew fitter, LACW Margaret Horton. In difficult windy conditions, Cox started his engine and taxied his aircraft to the run-up point near the runway; LACW Horton was following the customary practice of acting as human ballast, by lying across the leading edge of the tailplane, in order to prevent the aircraft nosing-over at high power while stationary. On completion of his engine functional check, the pilot taxied to the take-off point and, without realising that his human ballast was still present, commenced his take-off run. Cox soon noticed that the usually sensitive pitch control of the Spitfire had become exceptionally heavy and completed a, thankfully, brief circuit and landed safely, without any undue harm befalling his unwitting passenger. The aircraft involved, AB910, having first been delivered to the RAF in August 1941, is still flying today with the BBMF.

As one of the most highly-developed aircraft in RAF history, the Spitfire has appeared in many guises with a variety of weapons, both internal and external, and many appendages such as floats, skis, catapult attachments, and tail hooks: one extraordinary proposed modification was intended to enable this single-seat fighter to carry two passengers in addition to its pilot. In 1943, the Station Commander of RAF Biggin Hill, Group Captain Barwell, put forward a modification that would provide for the carriage of two people, one on each wing, of a Spitfire. The modification involved the use of a canvas-type material being fashioned into a shape that bore a remarkable resemblance to that of a body-bag! One of these bags was placed on top of each wing, and secured with a loop at its forward end being passed around the cannon barrel fairing; the rear end was fastened to the wing structure forward of the flap. It was not documented as having been tested with a live passenger.

Following on from a long-standing British tradition, dating back to the days of the Crusades, of presenting warriors with weapons and armour, the donation of a gift of military hardware became commonplace during WW1, when tanks and aircraft were donated by wealthy benefactors. This tradition was maintained throughout the inter-war years and into WW2: gift items usually bore the name of the donor in recognition of their generosity. In many circumstances, the aircraft or, exceptionally, the squadron that had been gifted, was itself renamed in honour of the donor, as in No 152 (Hyderabad) Squadron of the RAF, after his donation of a whole squadron by the Nizam of Hyderabad. A representation of the Nizam's turban head-dress forms the centrepiece of that squadron's official badge.

Lord Beaverbrook was a particularly strong advocate of public donation towards Britain's war effort. Whether this was purely a propaganda exercise, or a practical means of providing a worthwhile contribution to the production of aircraft is arguable; his 1940 appeal to the public, calling for them to support production of the Spitfire by donating their household aluminium pots and pans, as well as sums of money, was well-received and the response, magnificent.

For the purpose of Lord Beaverbrook's scheme, the price of a Spitfire was a nominal £5,000, although the true cost was around £12,000. Many towns, cities and organisations, as well as some individuals, all having donated the necessary sum, were recognised by their name or fund title being applied in four-inch high letters, in yellow, on the fuselage of "their" aircraft. Occasionally, the actual name-plate style was somewhat different from that of the official

MAIN
A Spitfire flies
over Duxford
Aerodrome in
Cambridgeshire.

MAIN
The "Sentinel" near the former Spitfire factory in Castle Bromwich.

Spitfire Notes and Anecdotes

version. Such was the success of the donation scheme that it has been calculated that around 1,500 Spitfires were presented in this way. The name-plate tradition has been revived by the present-day No 72 Squadron, two of their Tucano training aircraft being named "City of Leeds" and "Wings of Victory" after donated Spitfires.

The Spitfire lives on: it is now technically possible to manufacture a complete aircraft from scratch, such is the knowledge and expertise of those who have dedicated their lives to the unbelievably expensive restoration and, in some cases, the total rebuild of many examples of this iconic aircraft. It is also possible to purchase a flyable, 80 percent scale replica Spitfire, of which there are around 30 flying worldwide. For those considering the purchase of a Spitfire, be it a replica or the real thing, be warned, as for all things Spitfire, it will be expensive! The main limitation to the production of an authentic new-build Spitfire is in the engine department. Unlike the flyable scale-version that uses a car engine, there are few suitable power plants available for the full-size version. The Merlin, in any condition, is highly sought after, as is the Griffon. The "power" and the "growler" are in their element when performing their distinctive repertoire, and all airworthy examples have their flying hours carefully monitored so that the almost legendary aircraft, the Spitfire, can be kept flying, thus paying tribute to those who created, flew, and maintained her. Her place in history is assured, not only as a beautiful and effective fighting machine, but also as a symbol of hope for a nation in the dark years of conflict.

"If anybody ever tells you anything about an aeroplane which is so bloody complicated you can't understand it, take it from me - it's all balls." – R J Mitchell